COLOR YOURSELF CALM
100 PEACEFUL PASSAGES
TO COLOR

Thunder Bay Press
An imprint of Printers Row Publishing Group
10350 Barnes Canyon Road, Suite 100, San Diego, CA 92121
www.thunderbaybooks.com

Published in the French language originally under the title:
100 nouveaux messages à colorier – détente et apaisement
© 2014, Editions First, an imprint of Edi8, 12 avenue d'Italie, 75013 Paris, France.

All rights reserved. No part of this publication may be reproduced, distributed, or transmitted in any form or by any means, including photocopying, recording, or other electronic or mechanical methods, without the prior written permission of the publisher, except in the case of brief quotations embodied in critical reviews and certain other noncommercial uses permitted by copyright law.

Printers Row Publishing Group is a division of Readerlink Distribution Services, LLC. The Thunder Bay Press name and logo are trademarks of Readerlink Distribution Services, LLC.

All notations of errors or omissions should be addressed to Thunder Bay Press, Editorial Department, at the above address. All other correspondence (author inquiries, permissions) concerning the content of this book should be addressed to
Édition First, an imprint of Édi8, 12 avenue d'Italie, 75013 Paris, France.

Thunder Bay Press
Publisher: Peter Norton
Publishing Team: Lori Asbury, Ana Parker, Laura Vignale
Editorial Team: JoAnn Padgett, Melinda Allman, Dan Mansfield
Production Team: Jonathan Lopes, Rusty von Dyl

ISBN: 978-1-62686-660-7

Printed in China

20 19 18 17 16   4 5 6 7 8

COLOR YOURSELF CALM
100 PEACEFUL PASSAGES
TO COLOR

LISA MAGANO
CHARLOTTE LEGRIS

San Diego, California

Lisa's tips

With colored pencils

Using colored pencils allows you to create fine gradations, and to come up with your own shades by mixing colors. Soft pencils are best. The rule for a smooth color: always color in the same direction without going back and forth, and apply several light layers.

With felt-tips

The point can be large, medium, or fine: have fun mixing and matching! Just some advice: don't press the point too hard on the page, and don't go over the same area several times.

And a warning: felt-tips containing alcohol, whatever the brand, seep through the pages.

With watercolor pencils or marker

Simply color, then go over the area of your choice with a moistened brush to turn it into a watercolor.
Be careful—if the brush is too wet the pages will warp.
Remember to rinse your brush before using it on another color.

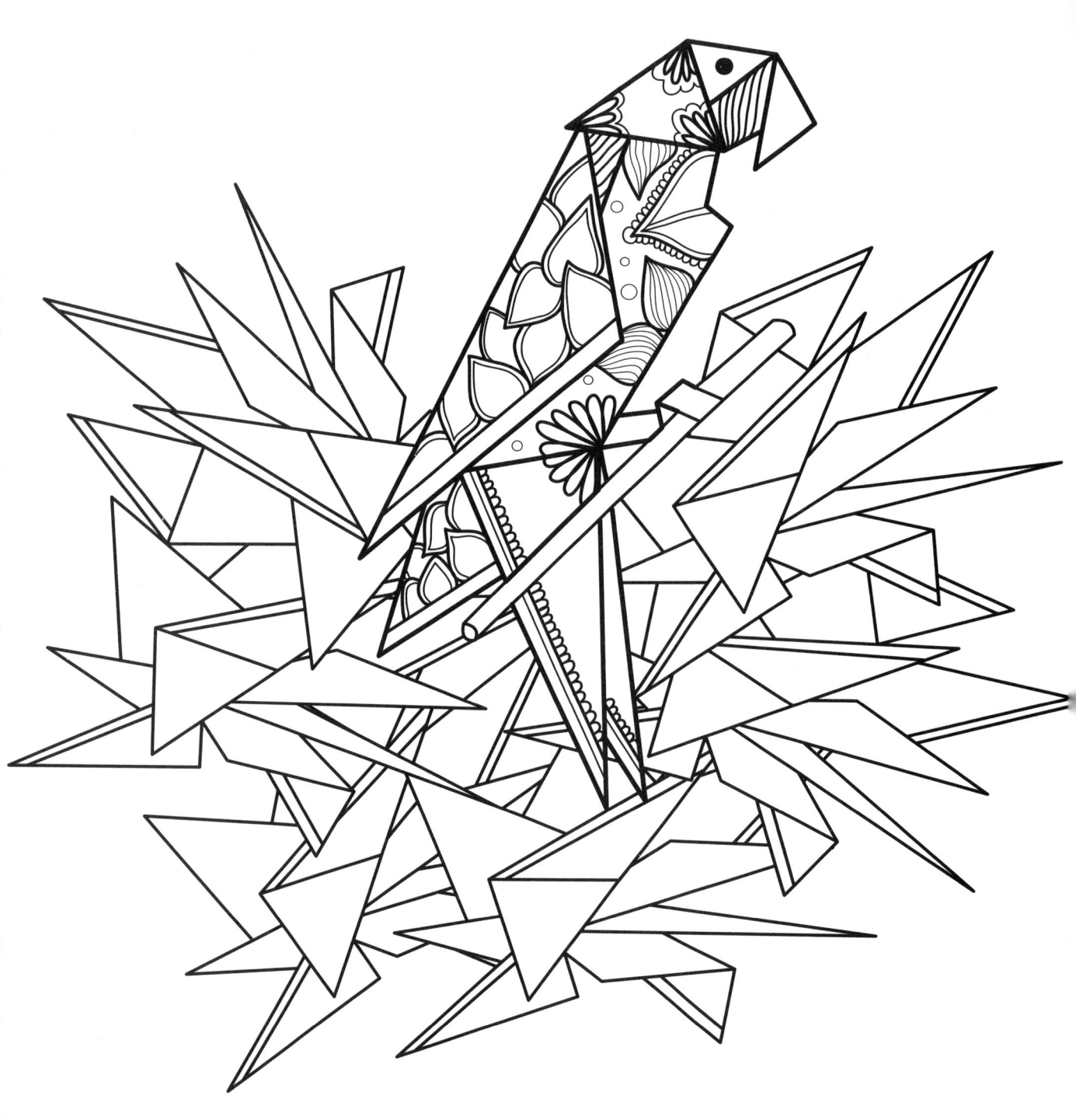

I am tiny and the universe is infinite.

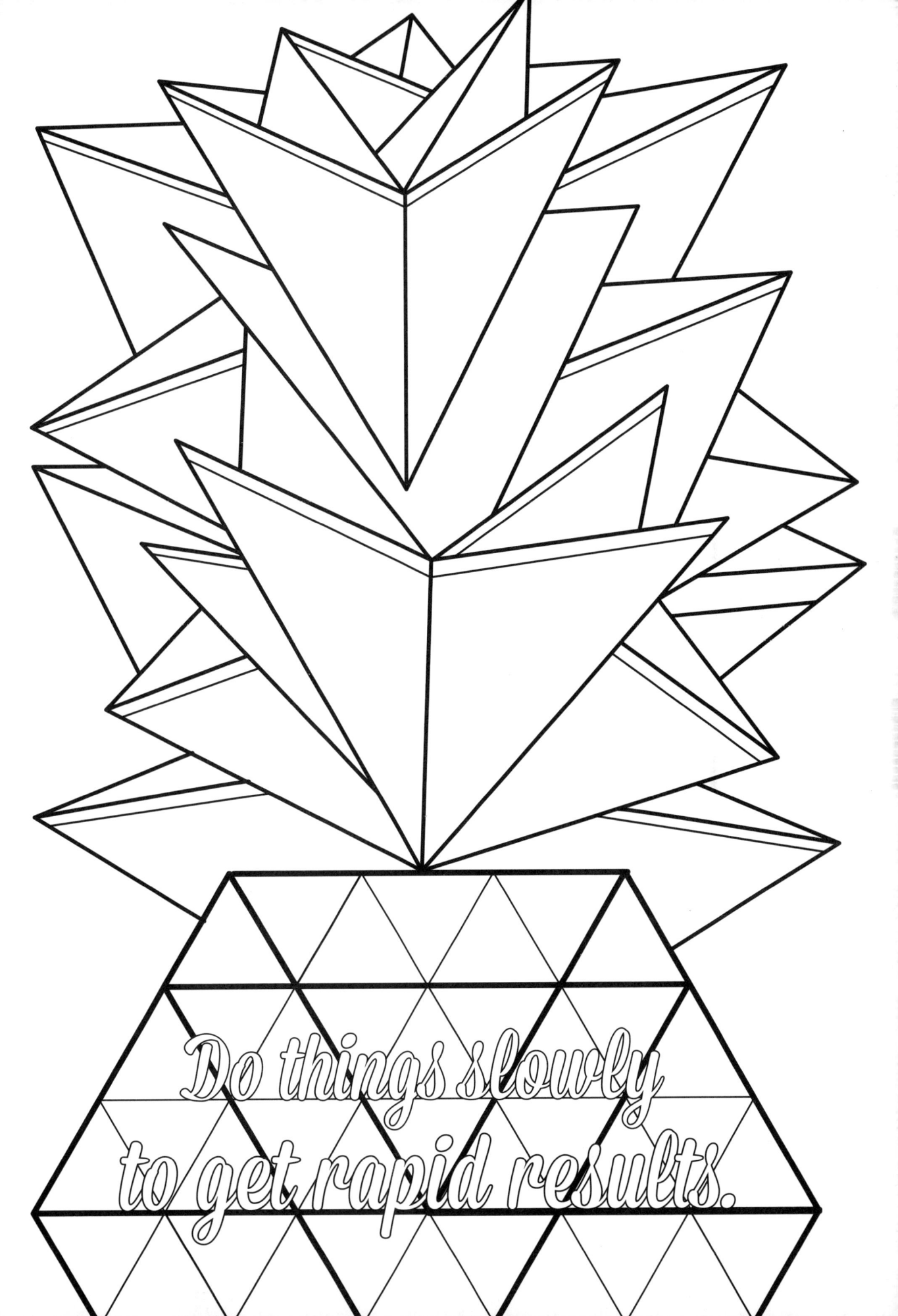

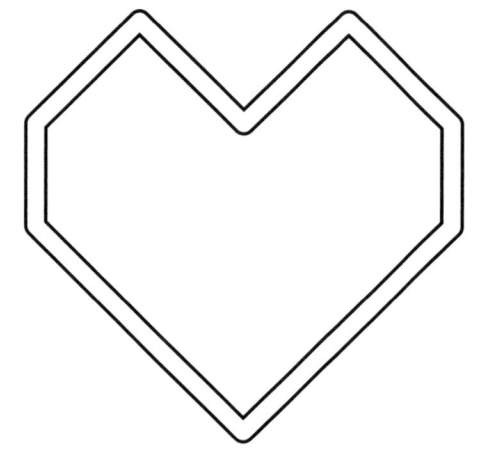

SILENCE WITH LOVED ONES IS NOT SILENCE.

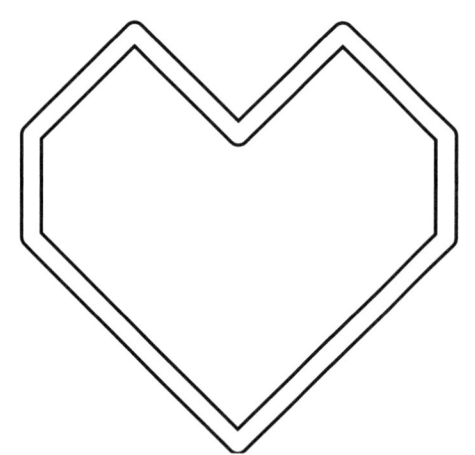

Look at the sky to elevate your soul.

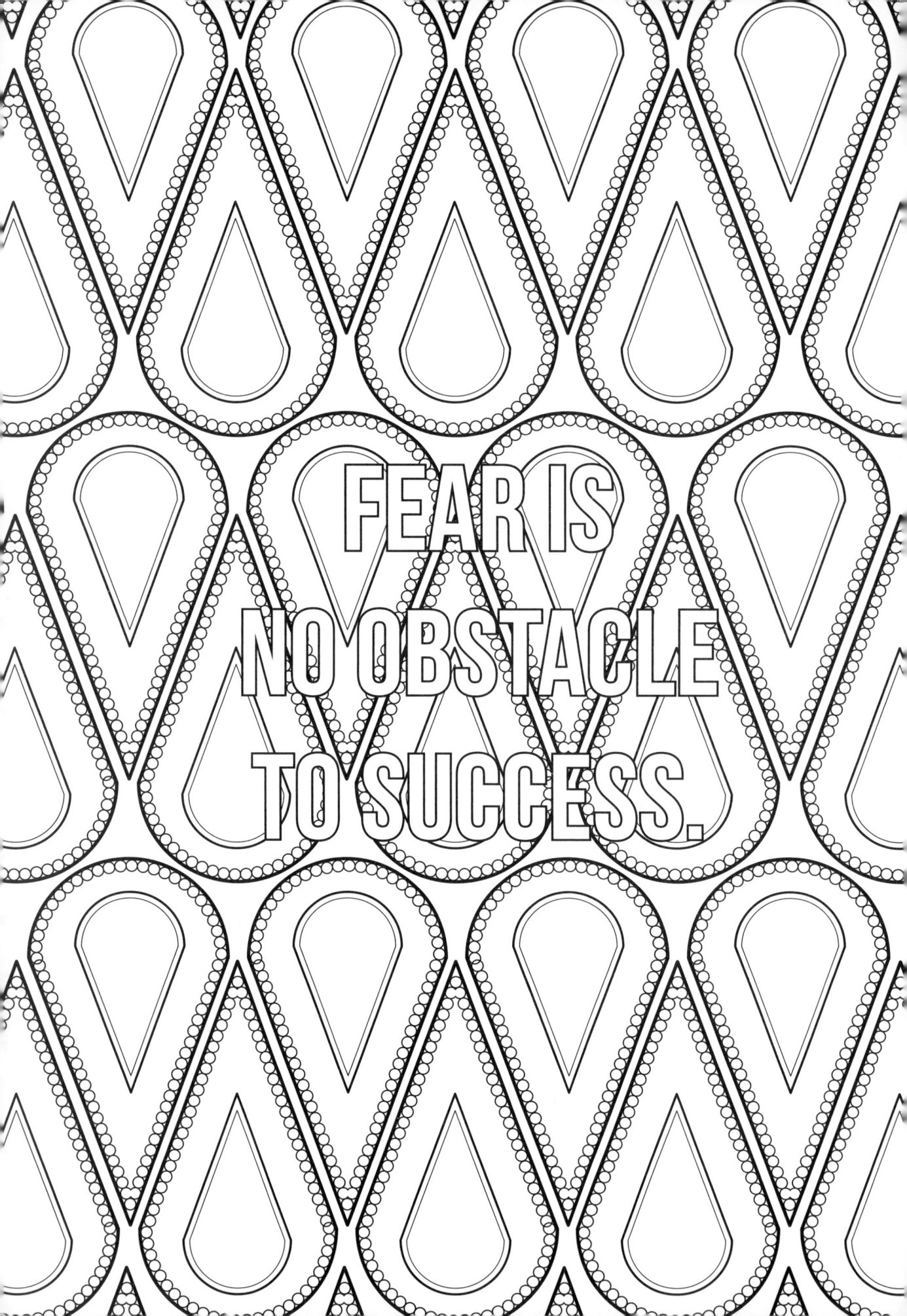

Calm is the ultimate refinement.

Re-create calmness each moment.

I sit on a bench and watch people go by.

The journey has just started and you are in charge.

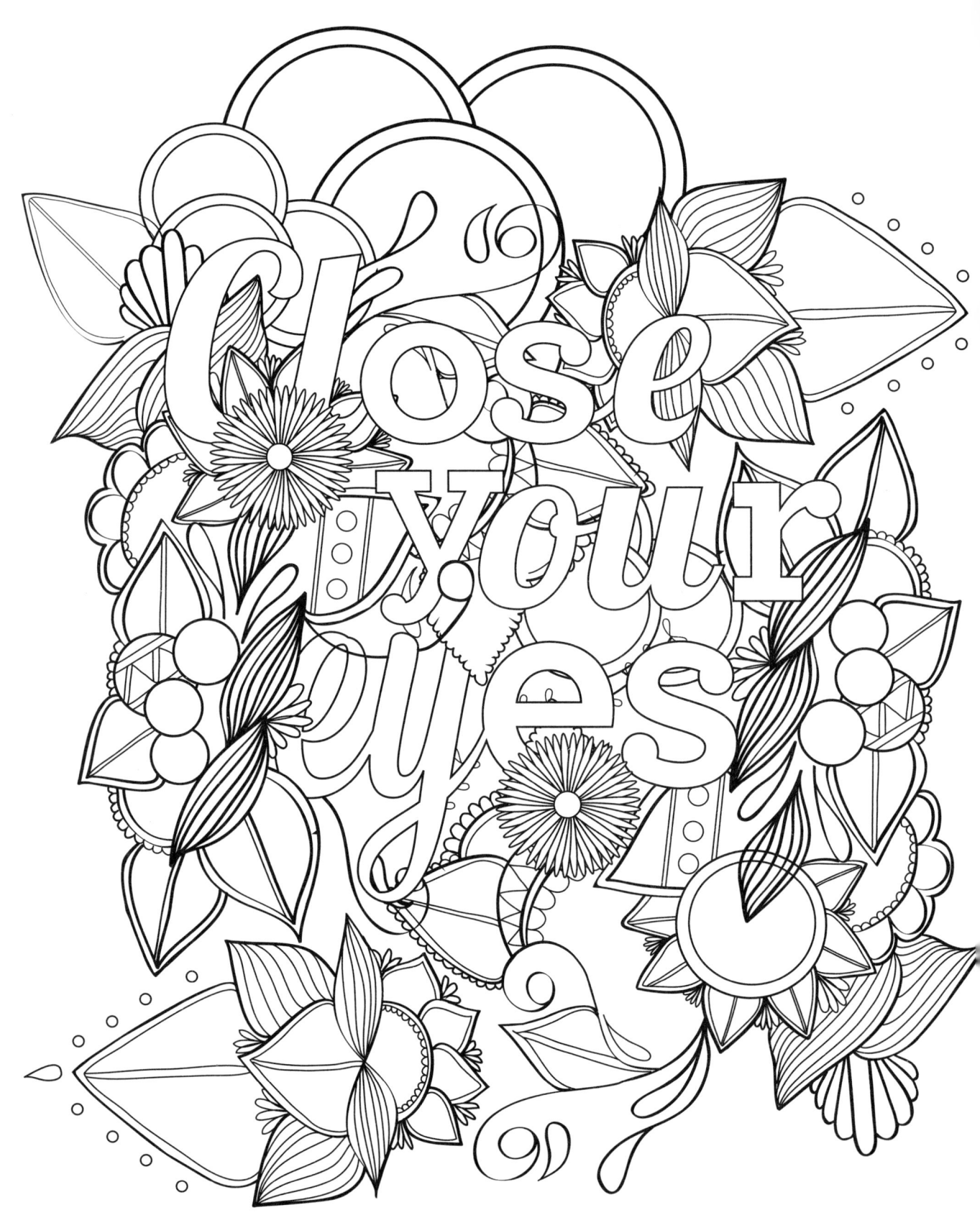

AZURE MIDNIGHT
Prussian
Cobalt STEEL CORNFLOWER
CERULEAN
INDIGO
BLUE
ULTRAMARINE
Turquoise

Today I have endless opportunities to receive.

Life goes along much better when you remain calm.

A moment of solitude is an opportunity.

I PUT ASIDE THE REGRET THAT KEEPS ME FROM HAPPINESS.

LEARN TO SAY YES.

I SEEK SILENCE IN MY SPIRIT.

Rest

Serenity
Stillness
Calmness
Quiet
Peace
Respite
Bliss
Silence
Tranquility
Relaxation

Who are people who comfort me?

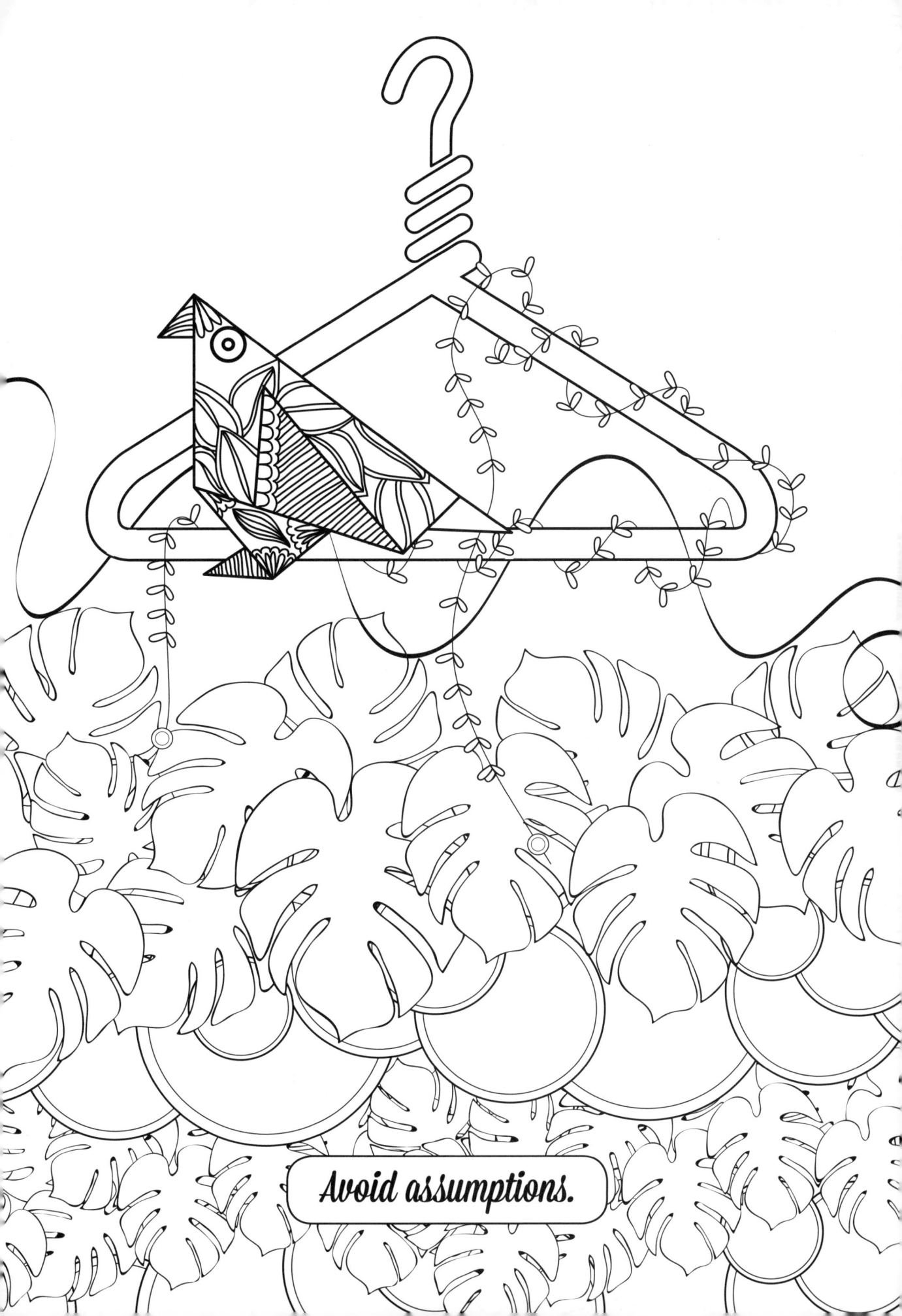

I get bigger by doing little things.

EXHALE
INHALE
EXHALE
INHALE
EXHALE
INHALE
EXHALE
INHALE
EXHALE
INHALE
EXHALE
INHALE

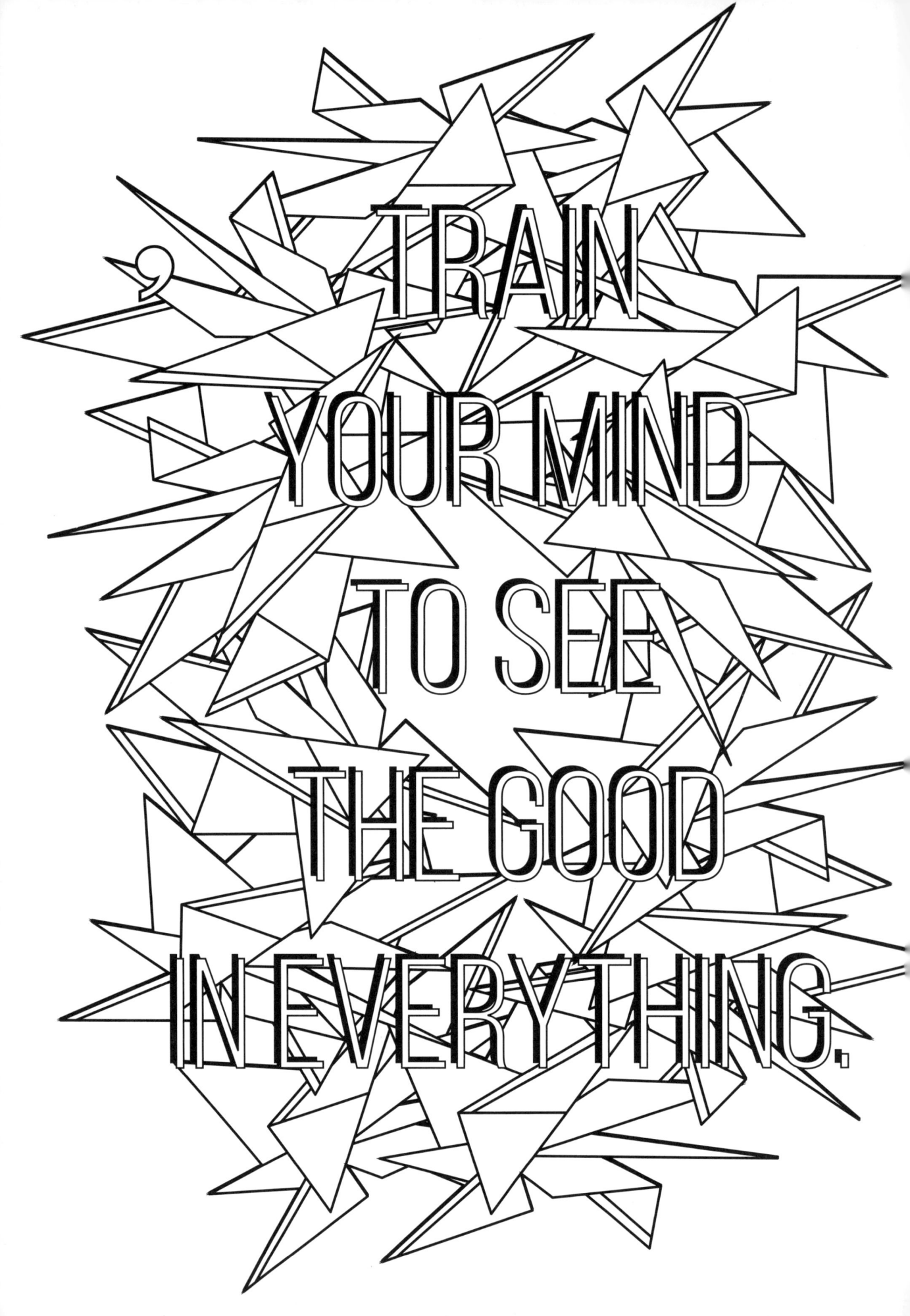

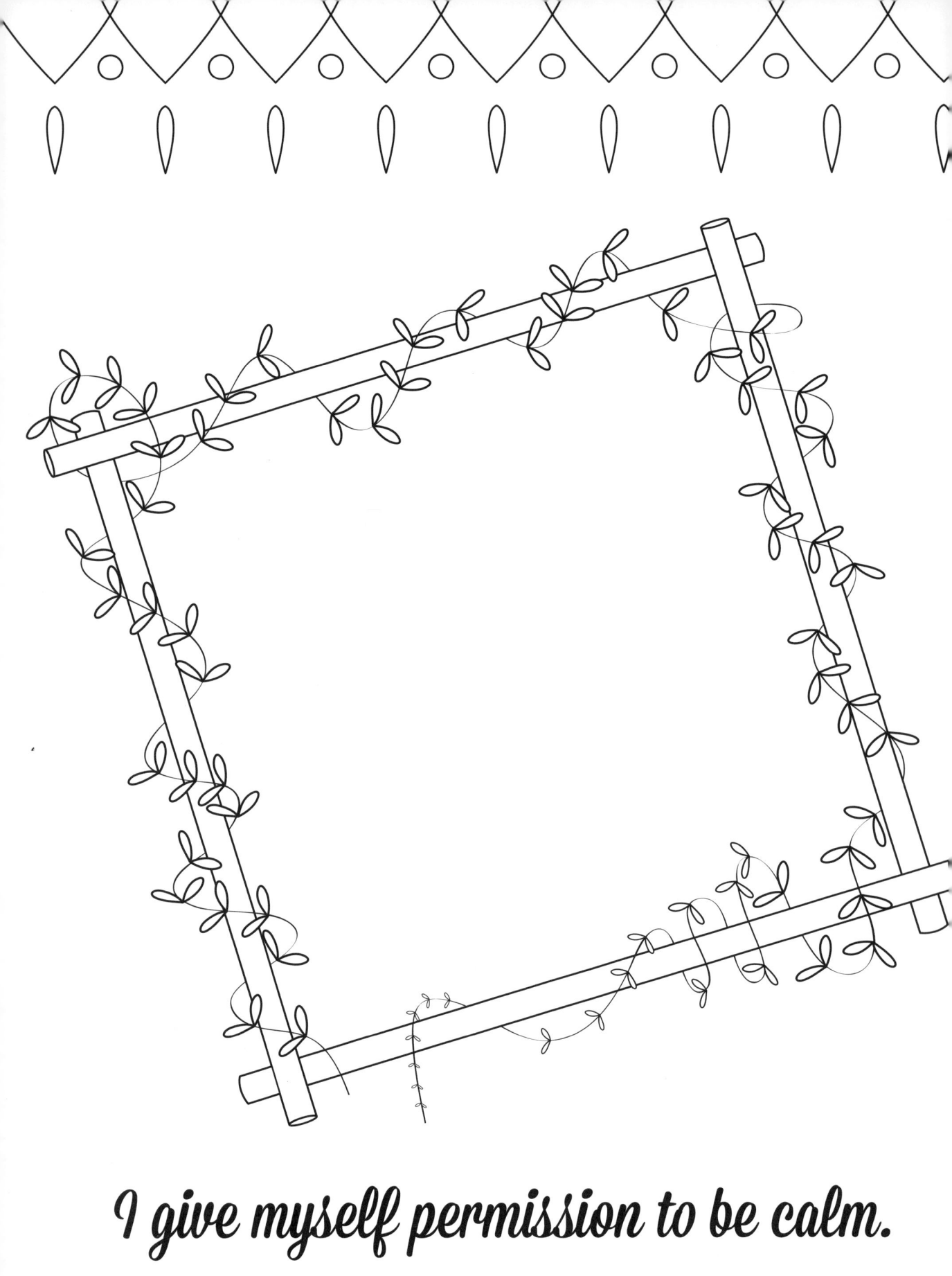

I give myself permission to be calm.

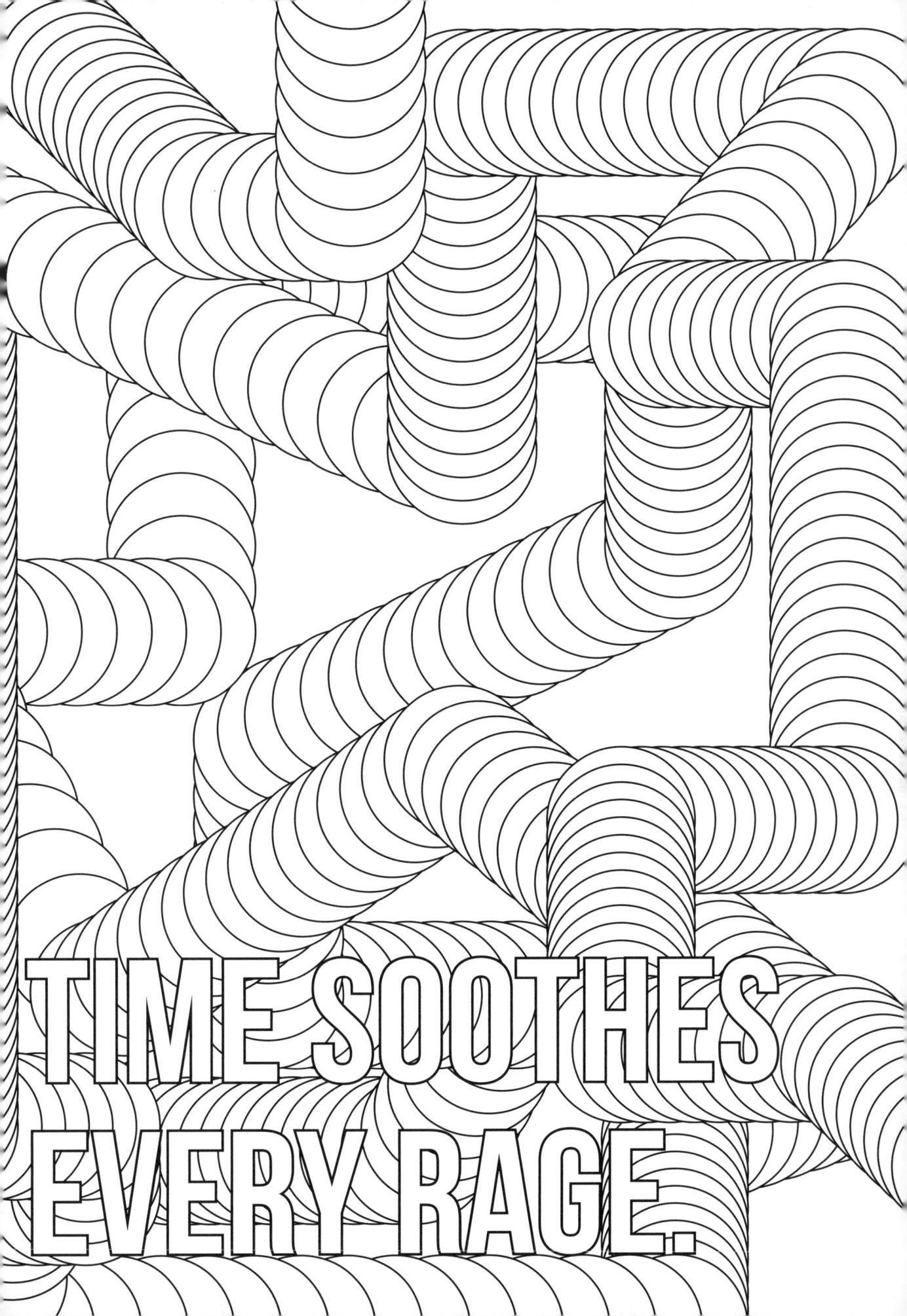

YOU CAN'T CALM THE STORM. YOU CAN ONLY CALM YOURSELF.

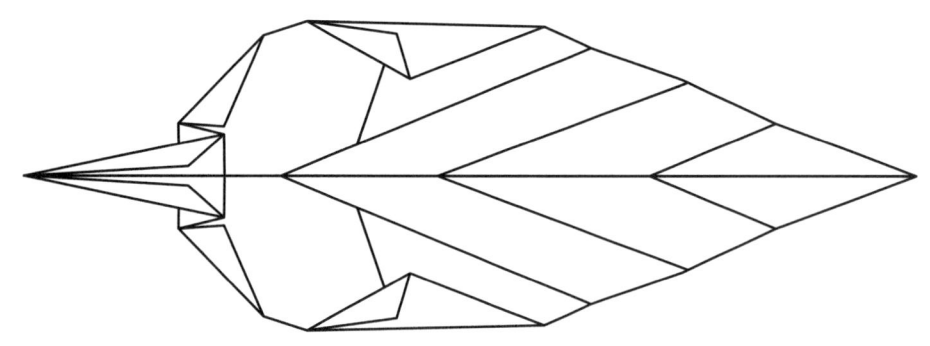

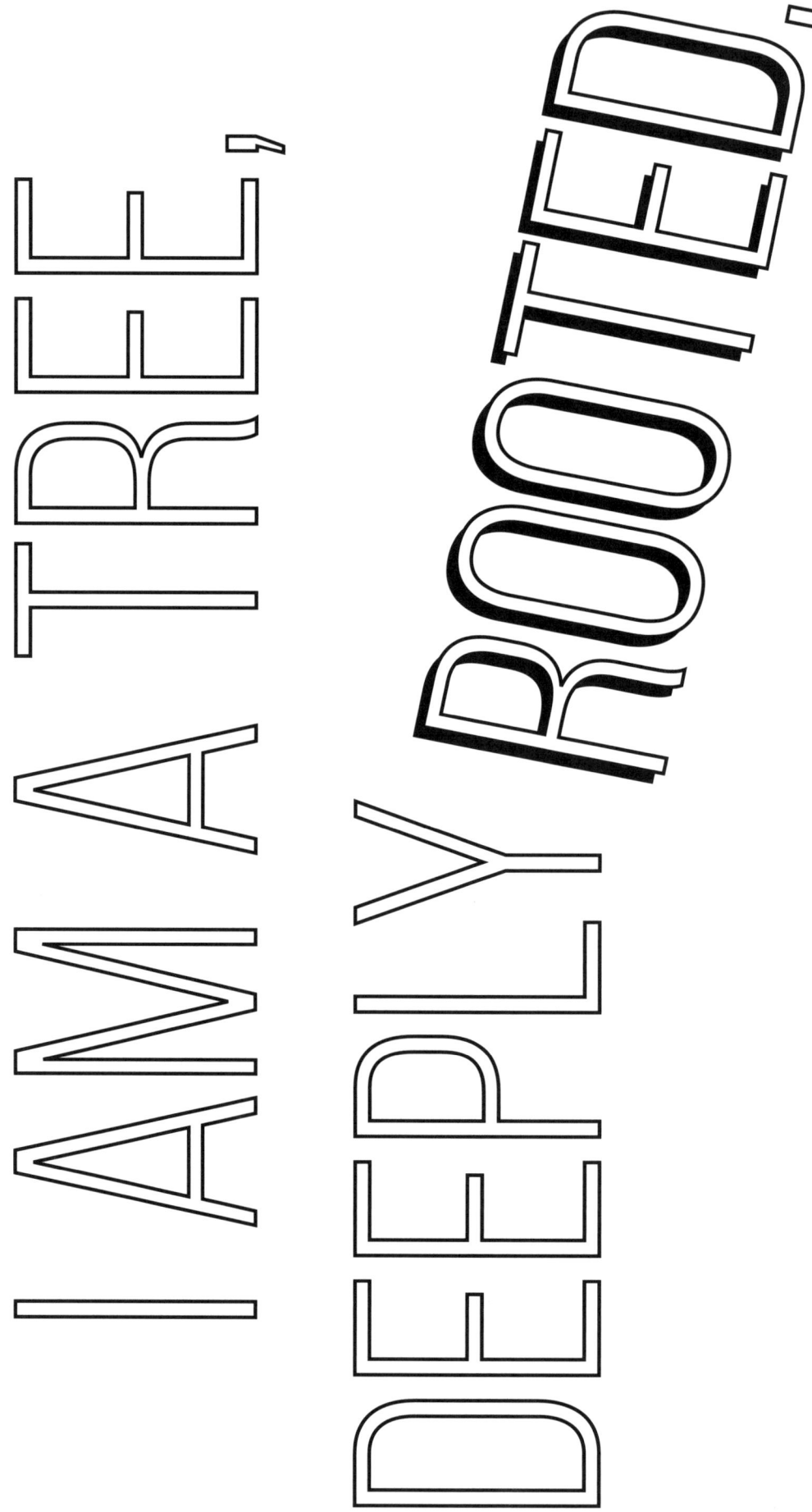

When my body is calm, my mind is calm.

Every flower is a mode of harmony.

Expect nothing of others except what you ask of them.

These are the colors of calmness.

MY MISSION:
MAKE
MY SERENITY
LAST
FOREVER.

WHEN YOU'RE AFRAID OF MAKING MISTAKES, CALL ON PATIENCE.

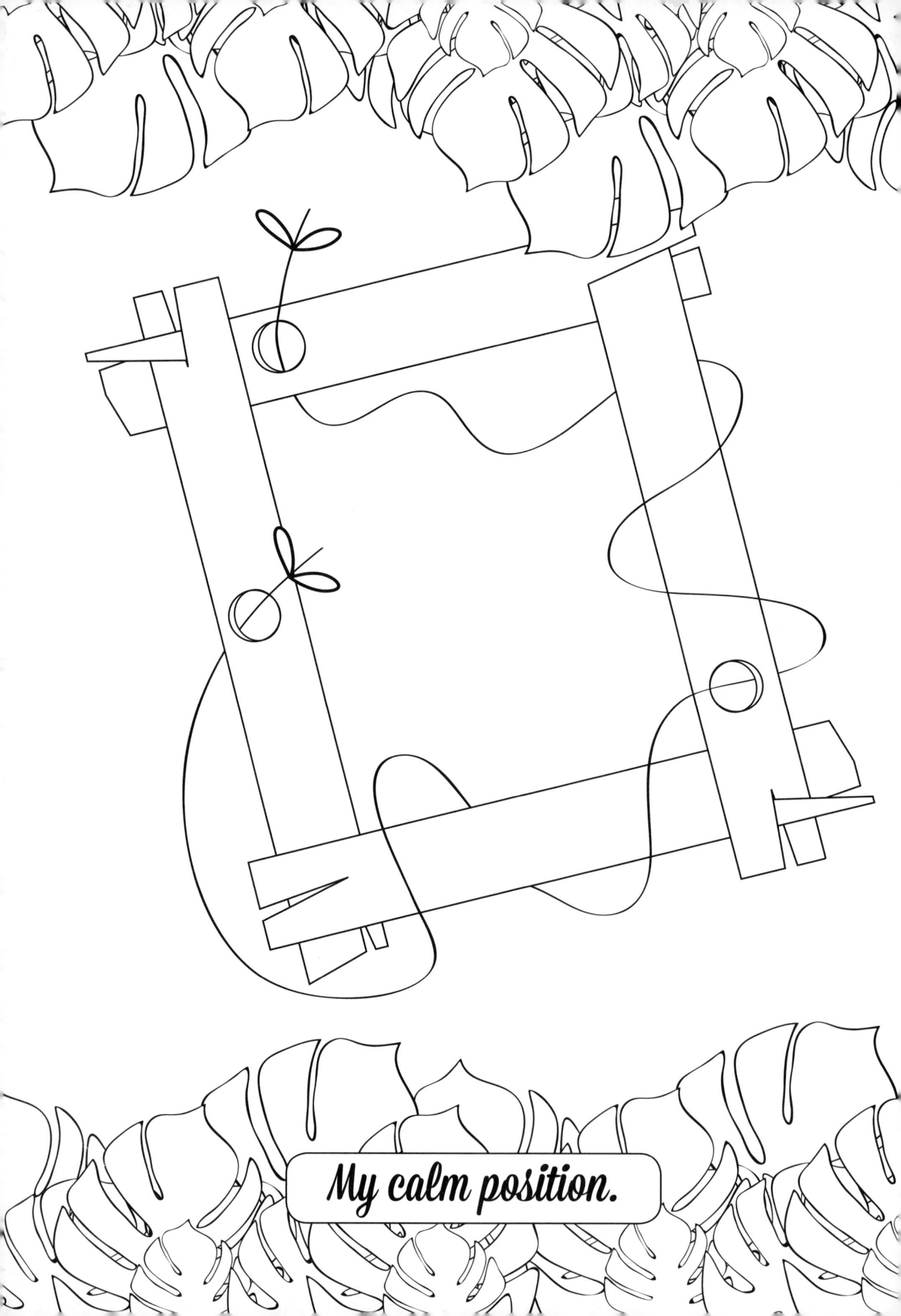

My calm position.

I WALK ON TWO LEGS: CALMNESS AND CONFIDENCE.

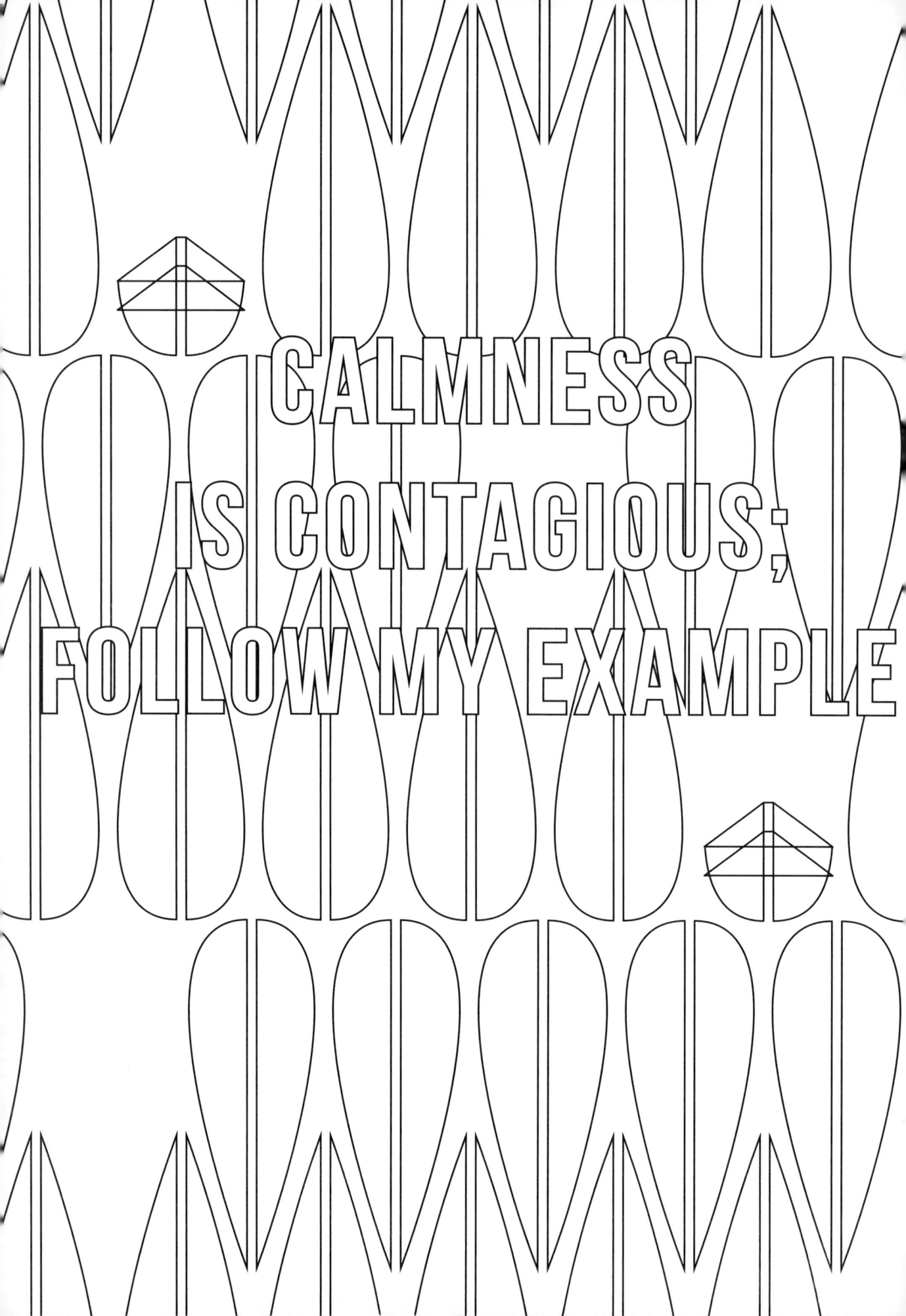

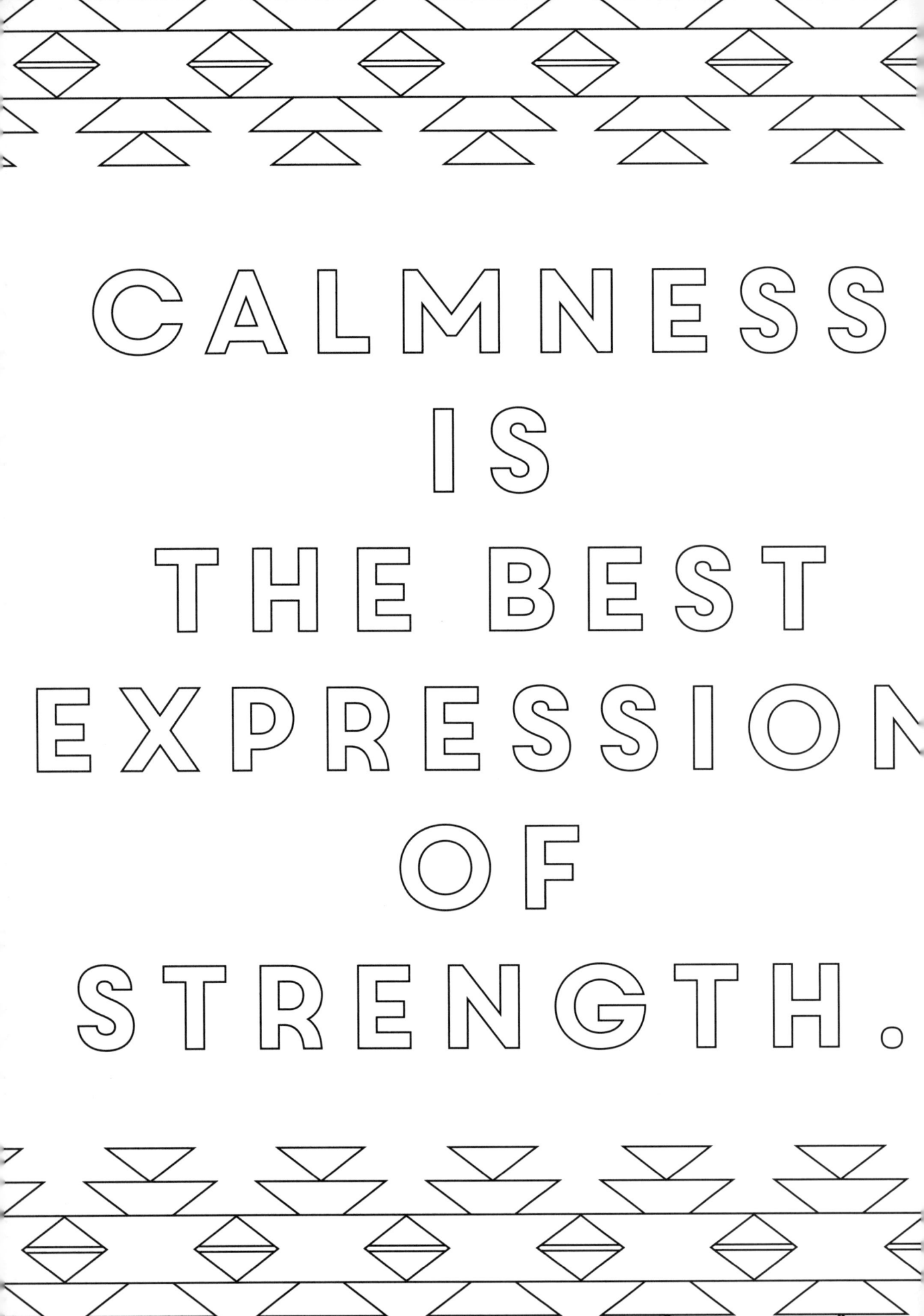

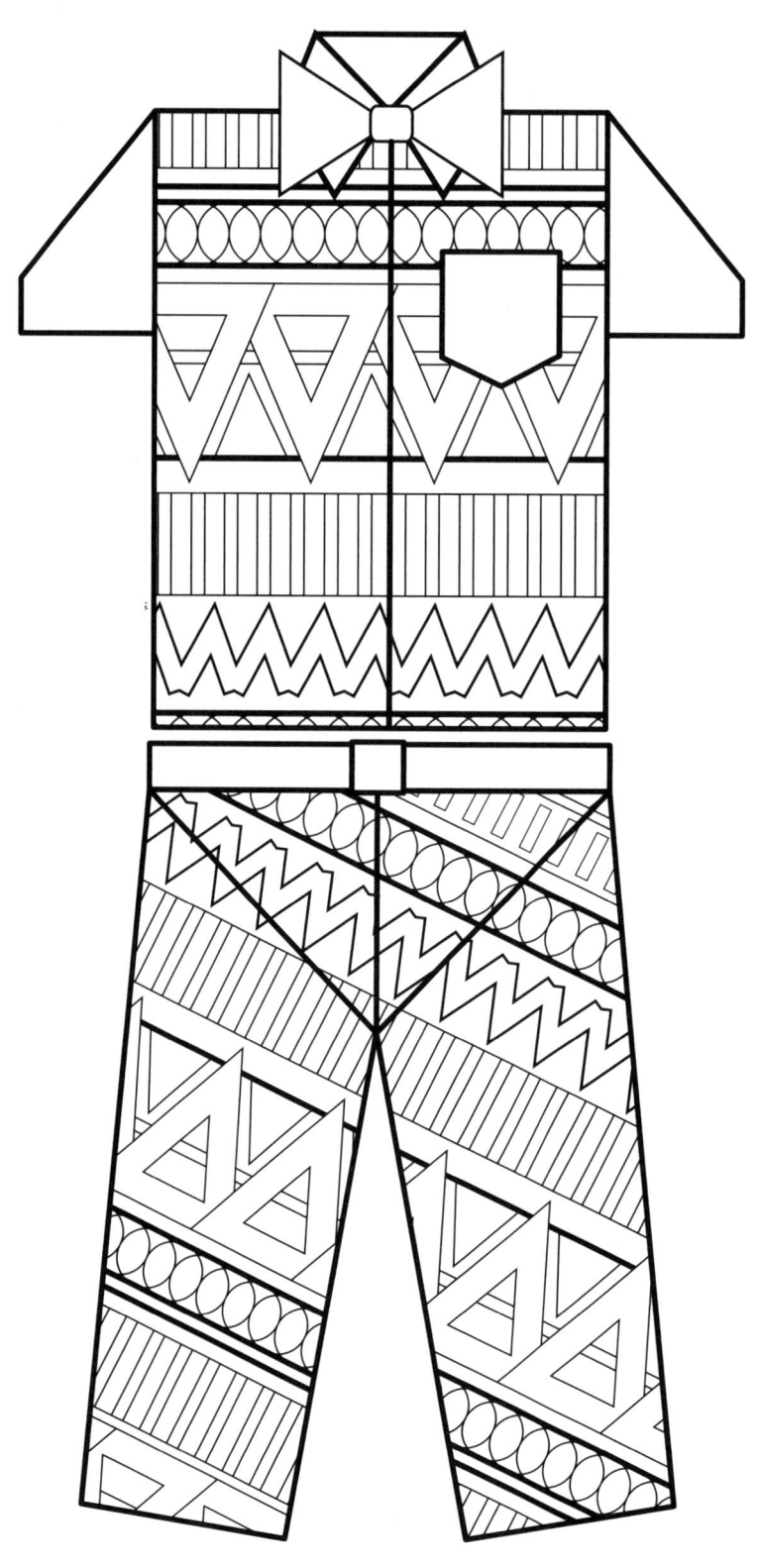

This is the color of a day without obligations.

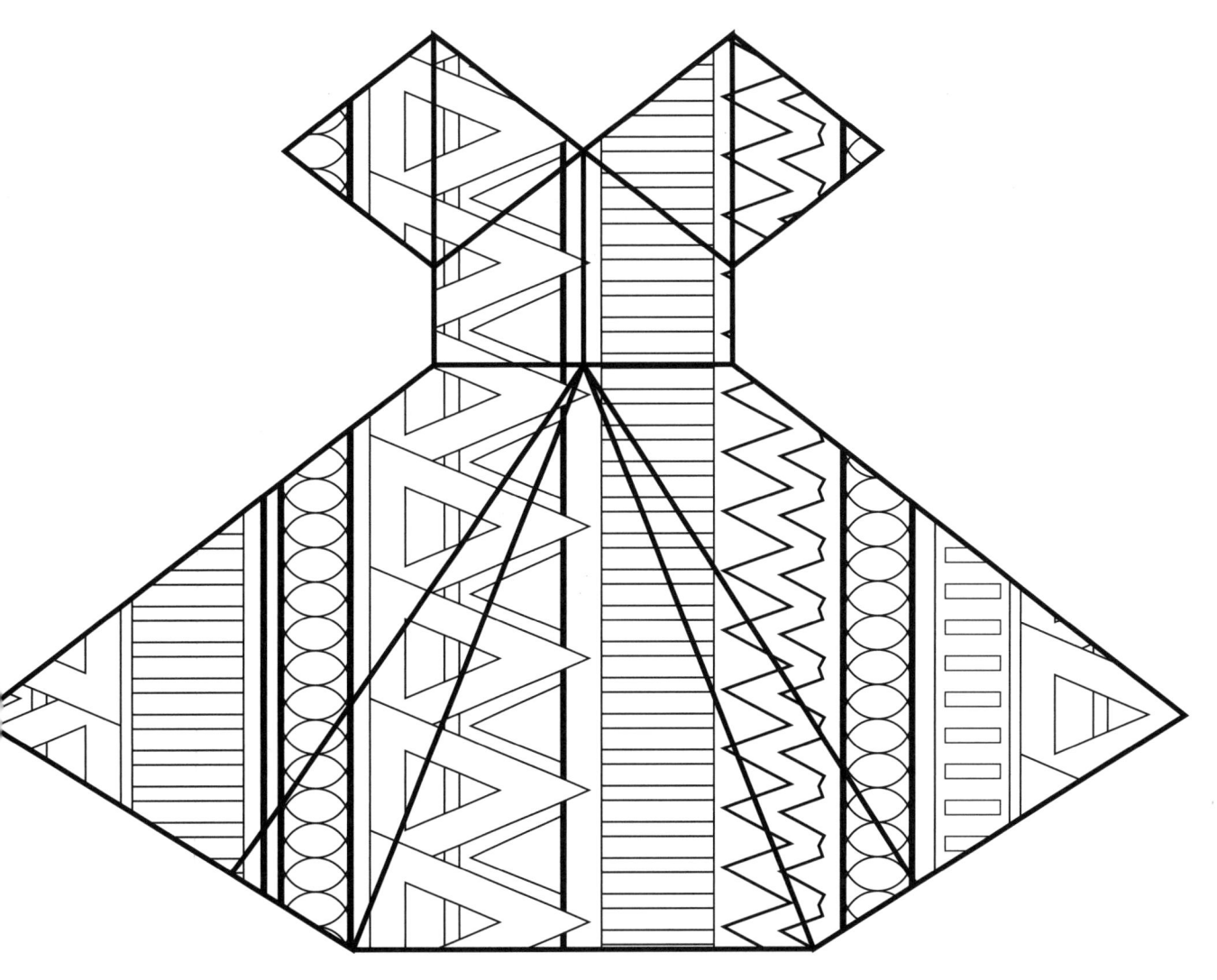

This is the color of a day without limits.

I listen to my heart beat.

I ASK MY INNER VOICE TO BE QUIET FOR A MOMENT.

I thank the anxious who teach me calmness.

Give away, sort...

You're the artist!